Growing Up To Be Mayor.™

The True Story of
Mayor Lee P. Brown

First
African American
Mayor of Houston

By Dr. Lee P. Brown
with Anita Higman

Illustrated by
Daryl Price

Published by

2204 Potomac Drive
Suite C
Houston, TX 77057

Design by
Concepts Unlimited
www.ConceptsUnlimitedInc.com

ISBN: 978-0-615-80607-5   (pbk)

13   14   15   16   17   0 9 8 7 6 5 4 3 2 1

Dedication

This book is dedicated to Mrs. Rosa Parks,
one of our heroes.

Table of Contents

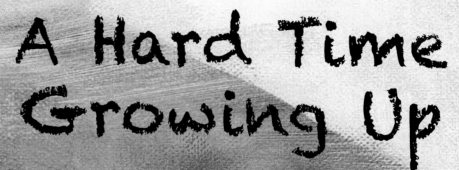

A Hard Time Growing Up

The truck engine roared. A little boy named Lee jumped up on the bed of the truck.

Other families with their children all piled up on top too. The vehicle was loaded down with all they owned. The families brought their clothes and food. They had to take pots and pans and bedding too. Whatever they could fit on the truck was stacked on top.

Lee tugged on his worn shirt. He squirmed excitedly, but he was also a little scared. Finally, the truck lunged forward. Someone waved and yelled, "We're off!" The truck chugged along westward on Route 66 at a slow and tiring pace.

Five-year-old Lee Brown rubbed his growling tummy. Lee and his family had lived in poverty in Wewoka, Oklahoma. They'd survived the lack of water and blowing dirt called the Dust Bowl. They'd made it through America's hard times of the 1930s. It had been called The Great Depression. But now their choices were gone.

Lee's parents were hard workers, but they could no longer make a living in Oklahoma. So the Browns, along with other African American families, were moving to California.

They believed better times were ahead. News had spread of California's rich land and lush crops. They'd heard that pickers were needed. Surely they would have work now and have plenty to eat.

On the trip, the heat raged like a furnace. Hours went by. The sweat poured. The days went by. The trip weighed heavily on all of them. After traveling through the plains and the mountains and the desert, they finally arrived. They were happy to be there in the lovely valleys of California. But it was difficult to cheer. It had been a long and weary journey.

A New Life in California

Now the hard labor would begin.

Lee, along with his family, picked grapes at farms near Fresno, California. Long days were also spent picking cotton and gathering up freshly dug potatoes.

Another job Lee and his brothers found was pitching watermelons. Workers would go out early in the morning and cut the watermelons off the vine. Then another crew would follow them around and line up across the field. They'd pass the melons along from one person to another and then up on the truck. Even though the Brown family was tired at the end of each day, they were glad for the work. Glad to make a living.

A New Home

The first real house had only one bedroom. The space did not hold the entire family. The boys, including Lee, slept outside in an army tent. Lee's family had no indoor plumbing. That meant all their water had to be pumped from a well. The family members had to carry in the water in buckets for drinking, cooking, and bathing. They used a large metal washtub to take their baths.

They washed their clothes by hand using a washboard. A washboard is a board with a bumpy metal middle. The person doing the laundry would scrub the clothes up and down on the ridges to clean them.

There were no indoor toilets either, so Lee and his family had to use an outhouse. An outhouse is an outdoor toilet that is inside a tiny building.

As Lee got older he had to get up early and help chop the wood. They used the wood to make a fire. This fire warmed their home and cooked their food.

Family Fun

Owning a bike like some of the other children wasn't possible because of the cost. But Lee did make his own homemade toys. He attached old skates to some wood and cleverly made his own scooter.

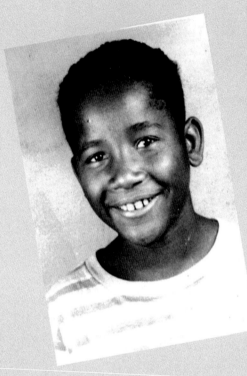

A camera was also one of the many luxuries that Lee's family couldn't afford. When Lee got older, he had his picture taken at the local bus station. He put a coin in the machine, posed for the camera, and out rolled a photo. This is one of the only pictures he had of himself in his youth.

Lee's favorite times were spent with his loving family. He enjoyed going to church and to the festive picnics that would often follow the services. His mother sometimes made homemade ice cream. Lee enjoyed cranking the handle on the machine. He thought eating the frosty treat, though, was even more fun than making it. Someone would holler, "The ice cream is ready!" And everyone would gather round.

A Chance for an Education

In California Lee entered school for the first time. To begin with he had only one teacher for all eight grades, and all classes were held in a one-room country schoolhouse. Lee did well in school. But prejudice against him because he was black became a part of his life. The schools were integrated. That means blacks and whites went to school together. Being black in America was not easy. But Lee's mother reminded him over and over that he was as good as anyone else. "No matter what negative things people say to you," she would tell him, "do not listen." So in the hard times, Lee remembered his mother's words and was comforted by them.

To Pilot a City!

Lee Brown's family never had the money to travel. Instead Lee explored many places through reading good books. Through the author's words he was able to imagine places he'd never seen before. Kids teased him, though. They'd say, "Lee is such a bookworm!" But Lee paid no attention to them. He just kept reading.

One of Lee's greatest inspirations was his mother. She insisted that he go to school. She told him if he got a good education, he could escape the cotton and grape fields. She told him, "You can make something wonderful out of your life." This encouragement stayed with Lee all through his years. When he hit roadblocks in life, he didn't stop. Lee always found a way around them. So once again, he remembered his mother's words and moved onward with his dreams.

While in high school, Lee's teachers also encouraged him. They hoped he would consider college and prepare for it with special courses. Lee followed their advice and was very grateful for their help.

Lee played football so well that he was awarded a scholarship to help pay his way through college. Once enrolled, he also worked sixty hours a week at a restaurant to help pay the rent, food, and fees. He got up at five o'clock every morning to mop floors and wash dishes. Later he worked as a cook and was paid one dollar per hour. Being accustomed to hard work and discipline helped him throughout his years of schooling.

Lee worked hard
to earn the money
to pay for his
college education

22

Lee Brown graduated and went on to earn three other degrees. He enjoyed a number of successful careers through the years.

After serving as the first African American sheriff in Oregon and Public Safety Commissioner in Atlanta, Lee Brown moved to Houston, Texas. He was Houston's first African American Chief of Police.

Lee Brown left Houston for a while to serve as Police Commissioner for New York City. New York City is the largest city in America. He also served as a member of President Clinton's Cabinet as the nation's first African American Drug Czar. As Drug Czar, he worked hard to stop the use of drugs throughout the country.

Left to Right:

Police officer in San Jose, CA.

First African American Chief of Police in Houston, TX.

Lee Brown loved Houston and called it home. This Texas city had been so good to him that he wanted to give something back to it. Lee said, "I want to make this fine city even better." So he returned to Houston to run for Mayor.

Being a candidate took long hours of hard work. Each person running for office had to convince the public that they would do the best job. Finally, the big Election Day came. The votes poured in. Everyone waited with excitement. Suddenly, Lee Brown had won! He was sworn in as Mayor in 1998 and became the Honorable Lee P. Brown! He became the 50th Mayor of the city of Houston. And he became Houston's first African American Mayor. He hoped by becoming Mayor that all races could look at city hall and say, "I too can become Mayor."

As Mayor Lee Brown led the city. He tried to keep everything running smoothly. Three of the many jobs he oversaw were putting out the fires, arresting the criminals, and making sure people had water.

He also made sure that the garbage was picked up and that people were able to get to the hospital when they were sick. The Mayor worked seven days a week. Sometimes he worked day and night. But the Mayor didn't do all of these jobs alone. He had 22,000 people to help him.

Most of the time Mayor Brown
spent his days at City Hall. He also went out into the
communities. Being among the people and sharing
with them was very important to him. He felt it
helped him to be a better Mayor.

Mayor Brown loved going to work every day because each day he could help someone. That was his favorite part about being Mayor.

Each day was different for the Mayor. He met people from all over the world. His days were full of meetings and activities to help the city and its people. Mayor Brown said, "I have the best job in the world."

However, not all days as Mayor were easy. There were hard decisions that had to be made. His choices were not always popular with all of the people. Some citizens complained.

Mayor Brown saw criticism as helpful. He did not take it personally. But instead he tried to see if there was any truth in what was being said. If so, then he had learned some new ways to improve his job.

Looking Ahead

Mayor Brown dedicated his three terms in office to the children of the city. So, he has a message just for kids. His wish is that every young person will be able to live out his or her dreams. A good education is important. In fact the Mayor believes it is the key to success in our society. Education gives a person knowledge and knowledge is power. That is the kind of power that no one can take away. "So stay in school"!

Mayor Brown wants all kids to have the same advantages he had through reading. He wants them to have access to lots of good books. That is one goal he pursued in his city. Mayor Brown believes his many years of reading helped him to become Mayor.

Among all the good things Mayor Brown saw, there is one thing that caused him sorrow. He was saddened when people from different cultures chose not to get along.

Being the victim of racism from childhood and even into his adult life, he knew how painful it could be. Mayor Brown recalled as a youth not being allowed to sit in a regular seat in a movie theater. All black people were forced to sit upstairs away from the whites.

These rules against African American people became known as Jim Crow laws. These rules began officially in 1875 and were meant to keep black people separate from whites. Blacks were legally forced to use separate public restrooms, separate water fountains, and separate seating in public places. These were only a few of the many senseless and cruel laws that southern blacks had to face even into the 1960s.

Mayor Brown believes that a person's color should not matter in America or anywhere. But it still does. He feels we have righted some wrongs over the years, but we still have a long way to go. There is good news, though. Mayor Brown also said, "I believe that people can change through understanding. By talking to each other and getting to know each other better, it is possible for all of us to get along together." Mayor Brown was very happy when Barack Obama was elected the first African American President.

Lee Brown knew hard times and rose above them. Even facing poverty and prejudice, Lee Brown always moved forward. With hard work, good values, and a strong faith in God, he went on to become the leader of one of the largest cities in America. He served three two-year terms as Mayor and has been given many awards and honors. He is an inspiration to all of us. Thank you, Mayor Brown, for a life well lived!

Dr. Lee P. Brown

Lee Brown's life has been one of vision, tenacity, commitment, hard work, and social consciousness. He has spent his professional career working to empower people and communities and to improve their safety, security, and quality of life. Cabinet member, educator, mayor, and author, his peers recognized his leadership when he was elected President of the International Association of Chiefs of Police and to the Advisory Board of the United States Conference of Mayors.

Dr. Brown's life is an inspiration. Born to migrant farm workers in rural Oklahoma, his birth certificate read, "Baby Brown." From that humble beginning, he rose to the pinnacle of American politics, serving in the Cabinet of the President of the United States during the Clinton administration and later as the first African American Mayor of Houston, Texas, the fourth largest city in America.

Dr. Brown worked his way through college and received the best public education this country has to offer. He earned a bachelor of science degree in criminology from Fresno State University, a master's degree in sociology from San Jose State University, and both a master's and doctorate in criminology from the University of California, Berkeley.

Dr. Brown started his police career as a beat cop with the San Jose, California Police Department where he developed one of the nation's first police community-relations programs. He served as Sheriff of Multnomah County, Oregon and pioneered the concept of Team Policing before being promoted to Director of the county's Department of Justice Services, a department comprised of all of the county's criminal justice agencies.

In 1978 Atlanta Mayor Maynard Jackson selected him to serve as Atlanta's Commissioner of Public Safety. He was responsible for the city's Police, Fire, Corrections, and Civil Defense Departments. After solving a high-profile case, he was selected by Houston Mayor Kathy Whitmire to serve as Houston's Police Chief and reform that city's troubled police department. Dr. Brown pioneered the concept of Community Policing and developed the Houston Police Department into one of the finest law enforcement agencies in the entire country.

Dr. Brown and his late wife, Yvonne, had four children and eleven grandchildren. His current wife, Frances, is a retired educator, having served for many years with the city's Independent School District. She is the mother of one daughter and two grandchildren. Dr. and Mrs. Brown reside in Houston.

About the Illustrator

Daryl Price

It was an honor to be chosen to participate in this book since the majority of my work as an artist consists of paintings of jazz and blues musicians with an emphasis on African-American history. The illustrations were an opportunity for me to see the American experience through the eyes of Dr. Brown and broaden my perspective as both an artist and as a human being.

Made in the USA
Las Vegas, NV
02 September 2021

29475456R00026